S'more
The Campground Kitten

BONNY GAFFNEY
Illustrated by Cecil Gocotano

To order additional copies of this book, contact:
Xlibris
1-888-795-4274
www.Xlibris.com
Orders@Xlibris.com

To my grandchildren—Ella, Peyton, Avery, Trevor, Liam, Harley, and Brynn—and to my husband, Michael. Thank you to Fred Gaffney and to Linda.

It was late spring, and without a warning,

five kittens were born one sunny morning.

One was much smaller than her littermates.
Would she survive? What was her fate?

When the monsoon came, bringing with it much rain, the kittens moved to higher terrain.

The small kitten tried to climb but got lost from the others

and was now on her own, with no sisters or brothers.

She was wet from the rain and cold from the night,

and the poor little kitten was losing her sight.

As her eyes crusted shut from some crud and some ick,

this little kitten knew she was sick.

She was hungry and tired, and needed to eat.

She found a large trash bin and jumped in with four feet.

Once she was in, she couldn't get out.

A lady camper came to see what the noise was about.

She took the small kitten, now tired, hungry, and wet,

to the manager who said, "She needs a vet."

Two little girls camping that same weekend wanted to keep her and make her their friend.

The girls named her S'more, and they took her away.

She went to the vet the very next day.

After two weeks of medicine and some fluids too,

the small little kitten was as good as new.

She found a new home that was indoors and warm,

and she'd always be safe from the next monsoon storm.

She had a bed to sleep on, some toys, and some food.

Then S'more, the campground kitten, knew that life would be good.

Printed in the United States
by Baker & Taylor Publisher Services